Drinks

Seed Learning

water

soda

tea

milk

lemonade

orange juice

hot chocolate

coffee

Would you like
some water?

Yes, please.

Would you like some milk?

Yes, please.

Would you like
some coffee?

No, thank you!

Word List

water

soda

tea

milk

lemonade

orange juice

hot chocolate

coffee